EXCELLING IN
BASKETBALL

By Heather L. Bode

ReferencePoint Press®

San Diego, CA

For more information, contact:
ReferencePoint Press, Inc.
PO Box 27779
San Diego, CA 92198
www.ReferencePointPress.com

LIBRARY OF CONGRESS CATALOGING-IN-PUBLICATION DATA

Names: Bode, Heather, author.
Title: Excelling in basketball / by Heather Bode.
Description: San Diego, CA : ReferencePoint Press, Inc., [2020] | Series:
    Teen guide to sports | Audience: Grades: 9 to 12. | Includes
    bibliographical references and index.
Identifiers: LCCN 2019003305 (print) | LCCN 2019009670 (ebook) | ISBN
    9781682826980 (ebook) | ISBN 9781682826973 (hardcover)
Subjects: LCSH: Basketball--Training--Juvenile literature.
Classification: LCC GV885.1 (ebook) | LCC GV885.1 .B644 2020 (print) | DDC
    796.323--dc23
LC record available at https://lccn.loc.gov/2019003305

CONTENTS

DO YOU WANT TO
BE THE BEST?

Teammates crept closer to the sidelines. Craning their necks, they watched the clock tick down the last few seconds. As the final buzzer sounded, the Fighting Irish of St. Vincent-St. Mary High School from Akron, Ohio, swarmed the court. Someone brought out a ladder, and the Fighting Irish ascended to slice the net from the rim. Back-to-back state championship titles for the team were a great reason to celebrate by cutting the net down. At the center of this celebration was a sixteen-year-old with National Basketball Association (NBA) aspirations. As a sophomore, he averaged more than 25 points per game and helped his team reach number 5 in

> "Every day, I go out there and work because there is someone out there working, too. If you stop, they can pass you up. My coaches push me, I push myself, my teammates push me."[1]
>
> – LeBron James

All the work that a team does during the off-season and in practice pays off during game time. The success can be seen when the buzzer sounds.

USA Today's Super 25. Wearing the net around his neck, he sat for an interview with a local reporter.

"Do you want to be the best?"

"Yeah," he responded.

The reporter continued: "I read somewhere you want to be the best defender, the best shooter, the best passer. What do you have to improve on between now and the NBA?"

"Getting stronger defensively and shooting the three."

Finally, the reporter asked about the pressure he faced as a star player: "How do you avoid complacency as an individual when everywhere you turn you're the man? The number one sophomore in the nation! What pushes you to get better?"

"Every day, I go out there and work because there is someone out there working, too. If you stop, they can pass you up. My coaches push me, I push myself, my teammates push me."[1]

That powerful drive, the sense of urgency, and the knowledge that competitors were working to surpass him helped LeBron James surge ahead of his fellow players. He went on to become *USA Today*'s and Gatorade's National Player of the Year as a high school junior and again as a senior. Then, without going to college, he entered the NBA.

From its inception, basketball has combined individual skill and coordinated teamwork. A variety of abilities must blend together. No one player can succeed against a team of five.

THE BIRTH OF BASKETBALL

In December 1891, when James Naismith was asked to invent a new game, it was meant to be a way of keeping the young men of Springfield College in shape between the football and baseball seasons. "We need a new game to exercise our students—a competitive game like football or lacrosse, but it must be a game that can be played indoors," said the school's Dean of Physical Education.[2] An indoor game that provided a strong workout without injuring players was Naismith's goal. The result became known as basketball.

Naismith originally wanted to use two 15-inch by 15-inch (38 cm by 38 cm) boxes as goals, but since none were available, the janitor gave him two half-bushel peach baskets. A soccer ball was used, and men were stationed in each balcony to help retrieve the ball if a "basket" was scored. Word of mouth drove curiosity about this new game, and spectators ringed the floor. The first public basketball game was officially held on March 11, 1892. One important spectator was Senda Berenson, the new physical education director at nearby

Smith College. She brought the game to her all-female school, and by March 1893, the first women's basketball game was held. Berenson officiated the game.

CHARACTERISTICS OF SUCCESSFUL PLAYERS

Following Naismith's invention, basketball players developed both as individuals and as teammates. While sports analysts, coaches, and players debate the most important characteristics of basketball athletes, a current National Collegiate Athletic Association (NCAA) coach says, "The ones who have done really well tend to be super competitive, have developed some fine skill and know how to *think* the game: share the ball, get the ball to the right spot, get their body in a position to gain an advantage, so there's a lot that goes into it."[3]

Although basketball was developed as a team sport, the individual players must develop skills on their own. This was intentional. Naismith wrote, "Its main purpose was recreation and development of certain factors that are particularly developed by games."[4] For Naismith, those factors included agility, accuracy, alertness, cooperation, initiative, skill, reflex judgement, speed, and self-confidence.

All of these are important in basketball today. They are developed by players who commit time to the sport. LeBron James knew what he needed to do to improve and excel at basketball. Players with similar aspirations can take the next step to learn to excel as well.

> "Its main purpose was recreation and development of certain factors that are particularly developed by games."[4]
>
> – James Naismith, inventor of basketball, on the reason he created the sport

CHAPTER ONE

WHO IS GOING TO
MAKE THE TEAM?

Before Michael Jordan had a line of Nike basketball shoes named after him, and before he helped lead the Chicago Bulls to six NBA championships, he was just another athlete trying to make a high school basketball team. "When I got cut from the varsity team as a sophomore in high school, I learned something. I knew I never wanted to feel that bad again. I never wanted that taste in my mouth, that hole in my stomach," Jordan said. "So I set goals of becoming a starter on the varsity. That's what I focused on all summer. When I worked on my game, that's what I thought about. When it happened, I set another goal, a reasonable, manageable goal that I could realistically achieve if I worked hard enough."[5]

The moment he got cut from the team changed the course of Michael Jordan's career. He could have given up playing basketball. There are those who face an obstacle such as he did and walk away. Jordan didn't. Instead, he immediately set up a plan to improve. After creating goals, it is important to work at meeting them by enlisting the help of a coach, watching and playing basketball, and improving individual skills such as ball handling, flexibility, jumping, strength, speed, and endurance.

Working to make the team starts long before tryouts. Players should use the off-season to improve their game.

THE IMPORTANCE OF SETTING GOALS AND PICKING UP THE BALL

Jordan knew what he wanted. But becoming a starter on his high school basketball team was much more involved. To improve in basketball, players need to set goals. A list of end goals is simple to write down. Figuring out the individual steps to achieve those goals is much more complicated and time-consuming.

Jordan's words give hints as to how he accomplished not only his original goal, but many more afterwards: He practiced during the summer. Summer is a prime time to improve individual skills. School is out of session and players often have extra time. Weather is favorable for finding an open basket at a park or in a driveway. The NBA season goes from October to June, so even NBA players take advantage of the summer season to improve their skills. "In today's NBA, summer has become the season when careers are shaped, new moves mastered and physiques honed," says *Sports Illustrated* senior writer Chris Ballard.[6]

A well-written goal will be specific instead of vague. Examples of vague goals are "I want to become wealthy" or "I want to be famous." Jordan's goal was clear, specific, and measurable. He knew whether his goal was reached when the starters for his varsity team were announced.

Goals need to be reasonable and realistic. For this, Jordan would have had to evaluate his skill set and figure out where he needed to improve, just as LeBron James did at the same age when talking to the reporter. Keeping a realistic perspective may have also included acknowledging that the coaches were correct in their decision to cut him. At the time, other players may have had a stronger skill set.

A basketball player's goals should be manageable within a set time frame. Jordan knew he had several months to train and improve before being confronted with trying out for the team again. He may have had a calendar on his wall where he could count down the days until tryouts.

Although Jordan did not reveal the specifics of what he did that summer, it most likely involved ball handling, shooting, and strength and agility training. These aspects naturally progress the more an athlete plays basketball, whether that means individually shooting at a hoop, playing one on one, or even three on three. Jordan took the first step: he picked up the ball. A college coach says, "Go get a ball. Someone is. If you're not, somebody else is. If you want to achieve your goal, then that's the most important part of it right there."[7]

Coaches provide structure and feedback to help players grow individually and as a team. Individual instruction can help a player to pinpoint areas to improve.

THE BENEFITS OF A COACH OR MENTOR

Anders Ericsson, a psychologist at Florida State University, described what became known as the 10,000-hour rule. This concept refers to the hours spent practicing a skill in order to master it. For example, in his research, concert violinists put in this many hours of practice to get to where they are in their careers. Winners of the famed Iditarod sled dog race also put in 10,000 hours of practice to master the skills needed for the race. Just like concert violinists have to master dexterity with their fingers, memorize their parts, and understand their role within the orchestra, NBA players have to master ball handling, learn the offense and defense, sharpen their shooting, and understand their role on the team. Players who have mastered these aspects of basketball have likely spent at least 10,000 hours perfecting their game over the years. But there is a catch: the 10,000 hours are not mere mechanical repetition. Shooting repetitively from the same spot for 10,000 hours will not make a player an expert at basketball. Ericsson said, "You don't get benefits from mechanical repetition, but by adjusting your execution over and over to get closer to your goal."[8] Ericsson suggests "deliberate practice" with a well-trained coach who can correct a player and lead them through a structured training schedule.[9]

Coaches provide feedback. This feedback serves not only to praise improvements, which builds self-confidence, but also to help identify errors so they can be corrected immediately. A coach watching for a hitch in a player's shooting motion can see it and stop the player to correct it. A player practicing solo might not notice it.

Coaches also provide a structured schedule. Players may be under the impression that a six-hour weekend practice is a great way to put in the hours. But concentrating on a specific task, such as free-throw shooting, for that long is incredibly hard. Eventually, the drill begins to lose its effectiveness. Coaches will alternate drills before players begin to lose mental focus. Science journalist Daniel Goleman says, "Learning how to improve any skill requires top-down focus. Neuroplasticity, the strengthening of old brain circuits and building of new ones for a skill we are practicing, requires our paying attention: When practice occurs while we are focusing elsewhere, the brain does not rewire the relevant circuitry for that particular routine."[10]

To get the best out of a practice session, it is not the length of time a player puts in, but the amount of focus applied while practicing that will help the brain retain new skills. When a player is paying attention to getting around a defender and focusing on the interaction in the drill, that intense practice is what helps build those connections.

THE POWER OF OBSERVATION

It is possible to learn and better one's self through the observation of others. This is also known as social learning. The basics such as dribbling and passing can begin with social learning. Whether watching a game from the bleachers or in front of a television, observation of other players makes connections in the brain so that when a similar situation arises, the information can be recalled without having experienced the situation first-hand. A legitimate way of learning while at rest is watching other players and taking notes on what they do. Players can create lists of their favorite stars along with their strengths. Many are envious of retired Los Angeles Laker Kobe Bryant's ability to adjust his body midair to avoid the defender on the way to the hoop. His amazing moves testified to his agility, core strength, flexibility, and spatial awareness.

BALL HANDLING

Breanna Stewart plays professional basketball in the Women's National Basketball Association (WNBA). But back in fifth grade, she was just another basketball player needing to improve her ball-handling skills. Always having been tall for her age, she figured she was destined to be a post player, working to make plays near the basket. Her father suggested she work on her ball handling. Stewart put headphones on, grabbed a ball, and made a routine of dribbling around the block four times each day, altering her dribbling hand each lap. "It wasn't a requirement, per se, it was more, 'Hey, if you really want to be good, maybe you should do this,'" says Stewart's father.[11]

Stewart was able to apply a fundamental basketball skill to her individual situation. The fundamentals of basketball do not change: players must be able to pass, shoot, dribble, and defend. But how dedicated players practice those skills is what sets them apart. Michael Jordan said, "Get the fundamental down and the level of everything you do will rise."[12]

Improving ambidexterity, the ability to use both hands with equal levels of comfort, is a benefit of consistently performing ball-handling drills with both hands. Stewart not only practiced with her dominant hand but also spent an equal time practicing with her nondominant hand. She removed the temptation to skimp on her left hand just because it was more difficult. Being a strong dribbler with either hand makes a player much harder to defend. It may seem that the basic ball-handling drills of "around the waist" or "figure 8" are mundane. However, there are ways to boost the level of difficulty. A partner can hold up several fingers to make sure that the dribbler's eyes remain up rather than looking down at the ball. The ball handler must shout out how many fingers she sees. Another idea is to practice ball handling with a player's eyes closed. Beyond that, NBA players have been known to have trainers toss tennis balls at them while they practice ball handling. They must catch the tennis ball with one hand while not losing control of the basketball with the opposite hand. Yet another idea is to practice the standard drills in "gears," just as a car starts in first gear and shifts into higher gears as it picks up speed. Players can start slow, in first gear, and gradually gain speed as practice continues.

FLEXIBILITY

Stretching before and after playing basketball increases flexibility. Being flexible is important because it increases range of motion at the body's joints and lengthens muscles. In basketball, that can translate to a longer running stride, allowing a player to sprint faster from one end of the court to the other. Flexible players display grace and finesse because of their ability to produce fluid movement. If injury does occur, flexibility can speed recovery time.

Prior to stretching, good warm-ups may consist of a low intensity walk, jog, or stationary bike ride. This should last five to ten minutes. Dynamic stretches should be done before basketball games. These include moving stretches such as ankle rolls, arm circles, neck rolls, shoulder shrugs, pendulum leg swings, side shuffles, butt kicks, and high knee walking. Dynamic stretches are stretches that are not held, but stretch the muscles as part of a movement. Static stretches are done after the game. These include chest stretches, elbows behind the head, butterfly, calf-stretches, and hamstring stretches. Static stretches are typically held for a duration to stretch the muscles.

While many young athletes tend to cut out stretching, it is suggested that athletes spend approximately thirty minutes stretching between pre- and postgame stretches. Some players, even LeBron James, take it a step further by practicing yoga. This not only helps with stretching muscles, but improves balance and control. While it may be hard to picture James in a reclined cow or one-legged pigeon pose, he takes it seriously. "Being on balance is something you should always keep in your game. That's a large part of the game for me," he says.[13]

STRENGTH TRAINING AND BALANCE

A player's muscles not only supply the power behind the movements they make but also serve as shock absorbers and stabilizers. As such, they help fend off injury. Think of how many times a basketball player jumps throughout a game. Including jump shots, defensive moves, and fighting for the ball on both offense and defense, this number is incredibly high. One wrong move, or even landing improperly, can sprain an ankle or rupture an anterior cruciate ligament (ACL). An injury to the ACL can end a player's season.

When trying to become stronger, a player can do many exercises using her own body weight or by incorporating basic exercise equipment such as medicine balls. Most often, this equipment can be found at a local fitness center.

Examples of strength exercises using a player's body weight include sit-ups, push-ups, pull-ups, abdominal planks, and lunges. Making these exercises basketball-specific can make them more challenging, but it will also translate into better performance on the court. When practicing sit-ups, a person can ask a partner to toss a ball so it can be caught at the height of the sit-up. Alternately, he can begin the sit-up holding the ball and pass it to a partner at the top of the sit-up. Then the partner can move so they are standing in a diagonal position in relation to the person doing the sit-ups. Repeating the tosses from a 45-degree angle activates the transverse abdominal muscles which run along the sides of the waistline.

Players should perform lunges, kneeling on one knee and stepping forward with the other leg. At each kneeling position players rotate at the waist from one side to the other. Using a basketball or even a light medicine ball, a player can toss the ball back and forth with a partner as he kneels and rotates with each lunge. This will work

Players can incorporate exercises such as lunges to help improve leg strength. Improving physical strength is a key part of getting better at basketball.

lower body large muscle groups such as quadriceps, hamstrings, and glutes. Adding the ball involves muscles in the upper body and core too.

To improve balance, the body's core must be strengthened. The main muscles in the core are the abdominal muscles. But the core extends all the way around the torso. Exercises such as planks and sit-ups can be key in improving core strength and balance. An additional idea, specific to basketball, would be to stand on a Bosu ball and simply play catch. A Bosu ball looks like a ball cut in half. One side is rounded while the other side is flat. An athlete can try balancing on either side of the Bosu ball. The ball produces instability in a player's stance, causing the abdominal muscles to work to regain balance.

Some exercises will be more challenging. Players should perform the most challenging ones first, when the body has more energy. They should control each motion rather than rush through each exercise. Slow and focused repetitions increase strength. Quick, jerky motions can cause injury.

INCREASING VERTICAL JUMP

When Deandre Ayton came to play basketball for the University of Arizona Wildcats in 2017, it was not just his 7-foot (2.1-m) frame that impressed the coach but also his amazing vertical jump. Measuring 43.5 inches (110.5 cm), Ayton's vertical jump stunned coach Sean Miller. "He's so physically imposing," Miller said.[14]

Ayton's arm span is 7 feet, 5 inches (2.26 m). Coupling his impressive frame with his vertical jump, it is easy to see how Ayton can block his opponents' shots and battle for rebounds above the rim.

Players may not be able to increase their height, but they can improve their vertical jump. This can be accomplished through executing plyometric exercises. To determine current vertical jump height, a player can stand with a shoulder against a wall. She should hold a piece of chalk in the hand closest to the wall. Next, she should raise the arm holding the chalk and make a mark with the chalk. Then she should bend her knees and jump, using the chalk to create a mark on the wall at the highest point. Measuring the distance from the first mark to the second mark shows her vertical jump.

Plyometric exercises not only increase vertical jump but also provide cardiovascular exercise. A third benefit is that they strengthen the bones. Jumping rope and dots are two examples of common plyometric exercises. Dots can be painted or taped onto the floor in an X pattern that looks like the five on a die. The person determines an

Box jumps help increase a player's vertical jump. This exercise strengthens the leg muscles.

order in which to jump—forward and back, side to side, diagonally, or any other pattern. Then the person jumps from dot to dot using one or two feet. A tuck jump is performed by squatting low and then bursting into a vertical jump while tucking the knees to the chest. Toe raises and calf raises are also beneficial in building muscle in the lower leg that can translate into vertical power.

PERIPHERAL VISION

Peripheral vision is the ability to see to the sides without turning the head. Peripheral vision registers in the brain 25 percent faster than central vision. Plus, peripheral vision aids the sense of balance. This makes a player's peripheral vision crucial in basketball.

In a game of one on one, the defender can concentrate on a single player. There is no need to worry about other offensive players receiving a pass. In actual game situations, when nine other players are moving, tracking players is vital. Staying low and positioning the body to be able to see the opposing team's players makes a player a greater defensive threat.

A common phrase barked by coaches at practices and in games is "see the floor." This means players must be able to locate their teammates and defenders and monitor their movements without constantly turning their heads. Think of headlights on a car: regular headlights illuminate the road directly in front of the car as it travels. The high beams illuminate less in the center and more on the sides of the car, allowing the driver to detect the presence of movement. Similarly, seeing movement on the floor is an important skill for all basketball players. On offense, it allows players to see which teammates are open for a pass or see a double-team coming. On defense, it helps predict ball movement, enables a defender to step in and help a teammate as needed, and lets players see opponents cutting to the basket. When in man-to-man defense, seeing the floor is done by opening the stance toward the ball slightly. This helps increase peripheral vision around the ball's movement and allows the defensive player to guard against incoming passes.

LeBron James, in analyzing one of his own game moves, says, "My main focus isn't

> "My main focus isn't on the guy that's guarding me; it's on the second level of defense, because I feel like I can get past the first guy who's guarding me."[15]
>
> – LeBron James

on the guy that's guarding me; it's on the second level of defense, because I feel like I can get past the first guy who's guarding me. But there comes a time where the weak side can come and [double-team] you."[15] Being able to see the position of multiple defenders without taking the eyes off the defender directly facing a player allows him to anticipate movement.

Eyes can be trained to improve peripheral vision. The key is to practice looking at angles of 45 to 60 degrees without turning the head. Dr. Larry Lampert, a sports vision specialist, offers this exercise that can be practiced with a partner and basic household items:

You will need a straw and two toothpicks. Draw a black line around the center circumference of the straw. Stand one to two feet in front of the straw, which is being held horizontally by the partner. Focusing on the black line, hold a toothpick in each hand and attempt to place them into the ends of the straw. Try to notice the ends of the straw with your side vision first. Again, relax your vision and be aware of the ends of the straw while looking at the center. Variations: If this exercise is too difficult at first, make the straw shorter. Once you master this exercise, make the straw longer by taping two straws together.[16]

SPEED AND ENDURANCE

A study published in the *Journal of Sports Science and Medicine* reported, "In elite basketball games, available time motion analysis research shows that adult athletes performed per game 105 high-intensity bouts."[17] Those surges to get open, cover a fast break, or box out for a rebound covered a distance of 0.6 miles (991 m), including fifty to sixty changes in speed and direction and forty to sixty jumps.

The study analyzed adults in elite game conditions, but the researchers also set out to determine whether training in intermittent high-intensity exercises could help junior basketball athletes. The study concluded that anaerobic exercises, which are short duration and high intensity such as sprinting and jumping, done intermittently within a regular practice helped athletes handle the cardiovascular demands of the game. This cardiovascular fitness is called conditioning.

While speed and endurance are partly genetic, all athletes can learn. "The anaerobic trainability increases with age (from childhood to adulthood with greater increases during puberty)," says the study.[18] This means that speed and endurance can increase as players grow.

From core exercises to sprints, there are many facets to physically preparing to excel in basketball. Stephen Curry of the Golden State Warriors says, "It's a high mountain to climb, but I'm pretty motivated to take on the challenge. Whatever that means, however you got on that mountain, why not try to climb it? And do it in your own way."[19]

THE DAY OF TRYOUTS

In the weeks prior to tryouts, players should check for open gym times. They should take advantage of these. One player says, "My freshman year, a week before tryouts, we had open gym shoot arounds. . . . The coaches would be there watching, but they weren't allowed to jump in and coach because it was still pre-season."[20]

There are several advantages to attending open gyms. It gives the coaches more time to evaluate players and it also allows players to build chemistry with potential teammates. Plus players should feel less stress at tryouts knowing coaches have already watched them.

Roger Kobleske, a high school basketball coach, spoke about how to get ready for tryouts: "Come with good shoes and socks.

When trying to make the team, there are steps that can be taken to help make that goal. A player can create a list of steps that can happen today, in one week, and in one month. A sample might look like this:

Today: Dribble around the block four times, alternating hands. Perform one set of dynamic stretches. Do a timed 50-m dash. Jump rope in sixty-second intervals. Play one on one. Perform one set of static stretches.

Next Week: Contact the coach and ask to meet for a training session. Continue ball-handling exercises. Continue stretching regimen. Alternate dot drills and jumping rope. Ask a friend to help with passing the ball during sit-up exercises and peripheral vision exercises. Time how long a plank can be held. Practice vertical jumps and record starting height. Invite more friends to play three on three. Make a list of personal strengths and weaknesses. Research favorite basketball players at a position and create a list of characteristics that make them strong players. Determine which characteristics from that list match personal strengths. For weaknesses, create a list of what can be done to improve.

Next Month: Meet on a regular basis with a coach or mentor to get feedback. Perform a stretching routine before and after active play. Ask a friend to video active play of a one-on-one or three-on-three match. Retime the 50-m dash. Perform timed planks, vertical jumps, sit-ups, push-ups, pull-ups. Record improvements and set new goals.

Be physically prepared by running, jumping rope, push-ups, shooting, and ball handling [work] on the weak hand. Coaches might explain what is expected and how many will be on the team."[21] Coaches and teams might vary on what they are looking for in a player. One player explains what this process is like: "I think one of the reasons I actually made the team was because I always tried to hustle."[22] And if a player does not make the team, they can know they gave their best effort. Michael Jordan says, "If it turns out my best isn't good enough, then at least I'll never be able to look back and say I was too afraid to try."[23]

CHAPTER TWO

HOW DO PLAYERS PREPARE
THEIR BODIES?

I n the early 1990s, whispers of a middle-schooler named Kobe Bryant reached the ears of Gregg Downer, a high school basketball coach in Philadelphia, Pennsylvania. Downer went to watch Bryant play. While it was hard to gauge the player's ability, Downer decided to extend an invitation for Bryant to visit Lower Merion High School. As an eighth-grade student, Bryant walked into Lower Merion's gym for the first time. He was approximately 6 feet, 2 inches (1.9 m) tall and weighed only 140 pounds (64 kg). "He looked like a lamp," Bryant's teammate, Rob Schwartz, says.[24]

ADOLESCENCE AND BASKETBALL

Kobe Bryant's height was increasing at a rapid pace, but the rest of his body had catching up to do. Taking good care of a developing body not only can increase on-court performance but also will establish healthy routines that can be carried forward into adult life. Adolescents who get regular physical activity and good nutrition also reduce their chances of developing risk factors for diseases such as high blood pressure, heart disease, type 2 diabetes, and osteoporosis. A growing teen is not just a smaller adult. The body of a growing teen has different needs than an adult's body.

Kobe Bryant worked very hard to become a physically dominant player during his career. But that dominance took practice and effort.

Teens not only grow their game in the off-season. They physically grow more too. David Epstein, former senior writer for *Sports Illustrated*, notes that as a result of more sunshine and its effect on human growth, "Children grow more quickly in the spring and summer than in fall and winter."[25]

The brain is developing during a player's teen years too. College coaches talk about a player's court IQ. This is not a physical skill, but a mental ability as it applies to basketball. Coaches look for a player's ability to read teammates, memorize patterns and plays, and remember scenarios and react accordingly. However, researchers writing for the *International Journal of Sports Physiology and Performance* note, "Memory skills typically mature after sixteen years of age and can take up to ten years to develop."[26] Just as a body's muscles and bones are developing and changing, so is the brain's capacity to remember.

With the onset of puberty, a person's height and weight will change. How weight is distributed often alters as the body matures. Athletes going through this stage of development may feel clumsy and off-balance. This happens because as height changes, the body's center of gravity changes too.

Rebecca Lobo, a former University of Connecticut stand-out and member of the Basketball Hall of Fame, says, "In fifth grade, my teacher told me that I needed to dress more like a girl and act more like a girl. . . . When I got home from school that day, I shot hoops until my parents returned from work."[27] By sixth grade, Lobo was 6 feet (1.8 m) tall and her dad showed support for her athleticism by never missing one of her home games. Lobo grew to be 6 feet, 4 inches (1.9 m) tall. With her family's support, and always listening for her dad's voice in the crowd, Lobo went on to win a gold medal with the US women's Olympic basketball team.

> **"In fifth grade, my teacher told me that I needed to dress more like a girl and act more like a girl. . . . When I got home from school that day, I shot hoops until my parents returned from work."[27]**
>
> *– Rebecca Lobo, Hall of Fame basketball player*

A HEALTHY DIET AND SPORTS NUTRITION

If a player feels as though she is moving in slow motion on the court, the cause may be poor nutrition. Eating a well-balanced diet consisting of whole grains, lean meats, dairy, fruits, and vegetables will provide the energy needed to sustain daily activities. Problems arise when adolescents consume too many sweetened beverages and too much junk food. Filling up on these items does not provide the body with needed nutrients and vitamins.

Sports nutrition differs from a well-balanced diet for a nonathlete. Playing a basketball game can burn about ten to eleven calories per minute depending on intensity and other factors. Over the course of an hour, that adds up to around 600 calories. Serious basketball players must take into consideration these extra caloric expenditures and compensate for them in their diet. When applied properly, sports nutrition prepares players for competition, provides fuel to maintain an active energy level during games, and offers recovery supplies for the body after intense exertion.

WHAT FOODS PROVIDE GOOD FUEL?

Carbohydrates provide energy. Carbohydrates can be found in breads, pastas, and potatoes. But they are also in vegetables, fruits, and even drinks. While readily available, foods with carbohydrates are not all equally healthful. Fast food might be easy to pick up on the way home from practice, but hamburgers and french fries can pack a lot of fat and sodium along with the carbs they provide. Foods that have carbohydrates and dietary fiber are better. The carbohydrates are more complex and give sustained energy. Simple carbohydrates are easily converted by the body to sugar, which gives a quick spike in energy before being stored as fat. Better options include whole grain

Food with good nutrition will help fuel the body. Athletes need to make sure to eat a good balance of carbohydrates, proteins, and fats.

bread, brown rice, or quinoa. Bananas, grapes, corn, and carrots are better choices than potatoes and french fries.

Protein is necessary to build and maintain muscle. Good sources of protein include lean meats such as turkey, pork, and fish, as well as yogurt, eggs, and tree nuts such as almonds. While many people already ingest adequate amounts of protein, basketball players training at a high rate will need to increase their protein intake. This will help with recovery as muscles repair themselves after hard workouts.

HYDRATION

To function at optimal levels, basketball players need to be well hydrated. Dehydration—a lack of enough water in the body—can negatively impact health and performance. To avoid dehydration, athletes must take precautions before the game even starts.

How much fluid an athlete needs is specific to that athlete. People sweat at different rates. The intensity of the workout and the weather conditions also factor into hydration requirements. If an athlete is experiencing thirst, dehydration has already set in.

Dehydration can cause a variety of physical symptoms. These symptoms include thirst, dry mouth, dark-colored urine, fatigue, headache, dizziness, and muscle cramps. If a player experiences any of these symptoms, more hydration is needed.

How do basketball athletes stay hydrated? "The general consensus is that it is better to drink water than to drink nothing during prolonged exercise in a warm environment, but drinks with carbohydrate[s] and electrolytes might promote better performance," says a study published in the International Journal of Sport Nutrition and Exercise Metabolism.[28] When the body sweats, salt is lost. Sports drinks contain electrolytes, substances that help balance water levels and blood pressure in the body. Such drinks can help restore a person's electrolyte balance. Consider the length of the basketball game when determining which type of liquid is needed. For games lasting under an hour, usually only water is needed.

Since hydration needs are unique to each individual, hydration amounts vary before, during, and after games along with a player's physical feeling. A general rule is to drink 16 ounces (473 mL) of water two hours before playing basketball. Then drink 4 ounces (118 mL) of water every 20 minutes during the workout. After the workout, drink an additional 16 ounces (473 mL) to replace lost fluids. Players should keep track of how they feel during all these stages, looking for patterns and areas where they may need more or less hydration.

SPORTS DRINKS, POWER BARS, AND GELS

A nutrition supplement is any food, powder, gel, tablet, or liquid that claims to have a benefit to physically active people. While student athletes should be able to maintain proper hydration and a balanced and nutritious diet without the aid of nutrition supplements, some athletes use sports drinks, bars, and gels to supplement their nutrition and hydration needs.

However, many sports supplement companies make claims that are not scientifically proven. There is also a lack of regulation when it comes to ingredients in sports supplements, and it is often left up to a product's manufacturers to regulate and test their products. A wide variety of ingredients across brands and types of nutrition supplements can make it difficult to find the right supplement.

Some parents feel that sports drinks contain too much sugar and sodium and have asked for them to be banned from schools. But these drinks are not meant to be consumed for regular day-to-day activity. Sports supplements are meant to replenish an athlete's body during exhaustive, high-energy work. Athletes are encouraged to try a variety of forms and flavors in advance of games or tournaments so they know what works best for them. A dietitian puts it this way: "You wouldn't be out looking for a new pair of shoes on gameday, would you?"

Quoted in Nik Streng, "Local Athletes Learn About Hydration," Argus Observer, August 22, 2018. argusobserver.com.

TRAINING TIPS

Having a written document stating personal goals is a good start in achieving those goals. For further accountability, a player can share personal goals with friends, family, coaches, or mentors. Physically keeping a paper with short- and long-term goals listed can serve as a reminder and as a checklist to complete.

Players can also keep track of personal statistics. They can shoot free throws in sets of ten and record the number of shots made. Information such as this also helps set new goals when original short-term goals are reached. Bringing a stopwatch or timer along to workouts can give players a chance to shoot baskets under the type of time pressure they might face during a real game. Stopwatches are also handy for timed sprints or for making sure equal amounts of time are spent on ball-handling drills with each hand.

What many players love about basketball is the competition. There are many drills and exercises individuals can practice on their own, but there comes a time when players want to compete. Playing with others and reacting to their moves is a great way to improve skills.

In high school, Kobe Bryant was known for calling his teammate Rob Schwartz at 5:00 a.m. to ask him to come over and practice shooting the ball. "And when I say go shoot, I would go rebound for him for an hour," Schwartz says. Other times it was half-court one-on-one games up to 100 points. Each basket was worth one point. "He was practicing real-game situations against me," Schwartz says.[29]

A current NCAA Division I coach says, "You need competitive settings because it won't always be a machine throwing a ball back to you exactly where you want it and you don't have to move. That's not how it goes in a game. That's why I suggest getting with peers and doing competitive stuff. Get your buddies with you to play one on one or two on two or three on three. There's a lot of fun games that organically emerge. There's 21 or shooting competition games."[30]

Even with the help of a coach or mentor, a player may never develop "perfect form." But some of basketball's most notable players became famous for just that: not having perfect form. Hall of Famer Paul Arizin was the first player to make the jump shot part of his regular repertoire. He was not trying to be creative. Instead, he performed the move out of necessity. "Because they held dances in

Games such as two on two can help players practice real basketball situations better than drills. Playing with a friend can also help keep practice fun.

those gyms, the floors would be very slippery. I couldn't get feet set under me to try a hook shot, so I started shooting with my feet off the floor," said Arizin.[31]

Another Hall of Famer, Rick Barry, shot free throws using the two-handed underhand shot known as the "granny shot." Barry was so accurate and reliable with this method that when he retired from the NBA, his .900 career free-throw percentage made him the best in NBA history.

The hook shot, a high one-handed shot perfected by NBA player and Hall of Famer Kareem Abdul-Jabbar, was very unconventional. It prevents the defender from being able to block the shot as the shooter arcs the ball overhead while keeping his or her body between the ball and the defender. Abdul-Jabbar said, "When you shoot it, you force people to wait for you to go up, and if they wait until I started to shoot it then they'd have to judge the distance and time it, and it's gone before they can catch up to it. That's, for me, the beauty of it."[32] Today the hook shot is rarely seen. "I used it to become the leading scorer in the history of the NBA," Abdul-Jabbar said. "There has to be something about it that works."[33]

"Napping is by far the most important and effective tool for coping with sleep crises."[35]

– Dr. William C. Dement, sleep researcher

As with individual drills, making a body conform to the perfect shot form may not be possible or even ideal. All players should make their shots personal. It is acceptable to have a form different from most players. A current coach says, "You look at players over the years and you see differences. If you have a reasonable form, a reasonably acceptable arch, and follow through, then the number one thing you can do is get reps."[34]

SLEEP

Sleep is integral to the body's ability to function at optimal levels. Sleep serves as a time for restoring the brain and body. Sleep is also a time when growth hormones are released. According to the National Sleep Foundation, teens need eight to ten hours of sleep per night, but many teens get less than that. This causes many to incur a "sleep debt." Feelings of lethargy continue as the week progresses until the weekend arrives and teens attempt to make up for sleep lost during the week. If late basketball games or early morning practices have a player feeling off, there are some suggestions that may help.

"Napping is by far the most important and effective tool for coping with sleep crises," says Dr. William C. Dement, a pioneer in

Having a good attitude makes a player a better teammate and easier to coach. This directly affects the team on and off the court.

the science of sleep. "Naps can make you smarter, faster, and safer than you would be without them," he adds.[35] Dr. Dement encourages what he calls "strategic napping." He found that a forty-five-minute nap increased alertness for the next six hours. Additional researchers found a one-hour nap improved alertness for the following ten hours. Keep in mind that the longer a person naps, the longer it takes the body to wake up. Any length of nap, even a so-called power nap, is beneficial. If a player has thirty minutes before practice, taking a nap may be a good idea.

PASSION VS. ATTITUDE

A player's passion for basketball can grow and change over time. Some players have grown up with a basketball in hand. Others grow to love the game due to environmental factors such as playing basketball with friends or with a school team. Whether a player's passion is already high or is still developing, presenting a positive attitude to others is important to success.

Naismith called attitude "self-sacrifice" and described it as follows: "In basketball there is no place for the egotist or for the one who is not willing to let another have all the credit if that will further the game. The unit in basketball is the team, not the individual player, and the one who would try to get glory at the sacrifice of the game is a hindrance to the team."[36]

Attitude is reflected on and off the court. Relationships with friends, teammates, classmates, coaches, teachers, and family can impact a player's attitude and alter their focus. High school coaches are often aware of a player's attitude, as they have access to the team's teachers, classroom grades, and behavioral referrals. A high school coach says, "A positive attitude is a smile on the face with determination to do one's best. Competing is a great learning platform. Compete hard, but always by the rules, acknowledging the efforts of your competition."[37]

It takes this positive lens for players to keep practicing and feeling the joy of playing. This is often called the love of the game. With that love of basketball comes dreams of future success. The top NBA draft pick of 2018, Deandre Ayton, tweeted, "I used to dream about getting an autograph from one of my heroes . . . now fans want mine."[38]

> **"I used to dream about getting an autograph from one of my heroes . . . now fans want mine."**[38]
>
> *– Deandre Ayton, Phoenix Suns 2018 NBA Draft first round selection*

COMMON INJURIES, CARE, AND PREVENTION

As with any sport, whether it be team-based or individual, there is a chance of injury. While basketball is not as physically rough as football or hockey, there are several common injuries that impact basketball players. These injuries are ankle sprains, ACL ruptures, and concussions.

ANKLE SPRAINS

Ankle sprains lead the list of most common basketball injuries. Ankle sprains often occur upon landing on someone else's foot or during a twisting and turning movement. While these incidences cannot be avoided, there are some factors that increase a player's chances of injuring the ankles. In a study reported in the *British Journal of Sports Medicine*, researchers studied more than 10,000 basketball players. They concluded that the greatest predictor of ankle sprains was if a player had a history of previous sprains. Players with a history of sprains were about five times more likely to sustain another ankle sprain. Another factor was not having proper footwear. This can impact a player's ability to move the ankle and foot correctly. A third factor was stretching. The researchers concluded that those players who neglected to stretch before a workout or game almost tripled their chances of suffering a sprain.

If a player suffers an ankle sprain, treatment depends on the severity. Many players with sprains need to see a doctor, while others can be assessed by an athletic trainer. Sprains respond to the rest, ice, compression, and elevation treatment. Once a player can stand on the ankle pain-free, a doctor or athletic trainer may prescribe ankle strengthening exercises and balance exercises. The use of ankle tape or ankle braces can help add support to a previously injured joint. Athletes may also want to consider visiting a shoe store to get assistance finding a shoe that offers the right fit and support.

> **"I jumped to a stop and it felt like my leg just separated in two. My upper body kept going while my lower leg remained planted."**[39]
>
> – *former high school female basketball player*

ACL INJURIES

The ACL is crucial to leg stability. Running diagonally through the knee, the ACL connects the tibia and femur. An ACL rupture can end a season. Two-thirds of ACL injuries occur without contact. When a player jumps to a stop, pivots direction quickly, or cuts into the lane, stress is put on the ACL. Women are up to eight times more likely than men to sustain this injury.

Part of the reason women athletes tear their ACLs more often is the quadriceps. Women are more likely to use their quad to slow down when running. This causes an instability in the joint.

"We had just come down the floor and the player I was defending received the ball. I jumped to a stop and it felt like my leg just separated in two. My upper body kept going while my lower leg remained planted," says a former player. "It was my senior year. I knew it meant my season was over."[39]

If an athlete wants to continue playing basketball, repair of the ACL requires reconstructive surgery and extensive physical therapy. Players can count on being out of competitive sports for eight to twelve months.

Because of the harsh recovery of ACL surgery, players and coaches should check knee stability. Knowing which players are at high risk for an ACL injury can help athletes and coaches determine a focus for training. A player's knee joints should be able to withstand the shock-load of the player's weight. To test this, a player can stand on a wooden box and jump off. If the player's knee or knees buckle inward, this shows a lack of strength and a susceptibility to injury.

To prevent this injury from occurring, Dr. Miho Tanaka of Johns Hopkins University suggests, "Data show that doing the right exercises can actually help prevent certain knee ligament injuries—like ACL tears—by strengthening the right muscles."[40] These muscles include the core and hamstring muscles. Tanaka says males tend to have stronger hamstrings than females. A common exercise to improve hamstring strength is the wall-sit. To perform a wall-sit, athletes stand with their backs against a wall. They place their feet about shoulder-width apart and slide down the wall while walking their feet out until the legs form a 90-degree angle. In addition to helping the hamstrings, wall-sits improve quadriceps strength and gluteus maximus strength. They are also easy to time, and it is easy to recognize improvement when doing them.

Imbalance in flexibility can also lead to injury, so Tanaka says to make sure both sides of the body are equal while stretching. An inequality can cause the body's center of gravity to shift, leading to injury. Exercises such as barrier hops done front to back and side to side, along with walking lunges, seem to be most helpful at preventing ACL injury.

CONCUSSION

Although football has the highest number of concussion-related injuries, concussions affect basketball players too. In fact, the highest number of concussions for female athletes occur in soccer and basketball. Concussions are traumatic brain injuries that impact memory and the ability to learn. Concussions happen when the brain

The wall-sit is a common exercise for many athletes. It can help with core and hamstring strength.

forcefully strikes the inside of the skull. Their diagnosis and treatment should be taken seriously.

Concussions can happen while diving for a loose ball, during a midair collision, or after slamming into a gym wall. They can also occur by experiencing a fall or an indirect hit on any other part of the body. There does not have to be a direct blow to the head for a concussion to occur. Medical professionals say a concussion can occur with or without a loss of consciousness.

Many sports leagues and high school teams now require education on concussions. Coaches are taught the "When in doubt, sit them out" slogan because an estimated 170,000 children and teens are treated in emergency rooms for concussion and other brain-related injuries on an annual basis.

Concussion symptoms include, but are not limited to, headache, dizziness, nausea, balance problems, fatigue, drowsiness, sensitivity to light and noise, and irritability. Due to the wide variety of possible symptoms, in 2018 the Centers for Disease Control and Prevention issued new guidelines specifically addressing concussion in children and adolescents. Dr. Ed Benzel helped create the new guidelines. He says, "It's going to increase and further heighten our awareness regarding potential injuries and how to manage them and how to prevent them. We want to make sure that kids don't return to play too soon and incur another injury which is much more severe."[41]

If players have ever had a concussion, they are at greater risk for another one. Since teens' and children's brains are still developing, it is important that the athlete receive a complete physical and cognitive recovery and medical clearance to return before reentering sports programs. This may mean complete absence from school or a shortened-day schedule. Physical activity should be completely stopped for at least twenty-four hours and then, depending on the severity of the concussion, can be gradually resumed. Typical recovery time for a concussion is approximately seven days but can take longer, sometimes even weeks or months.

MAKING THE MOST OF BEING SIDELINED

Being injured and having to sit out can be a challenge. It is important to recover and get healthy, but players may be anxious to return to the team and contribute. Depending on the severity of a player's injury, there may be activities a player can still do to participate and support the team.

For example, if a player has a lower body injury, upper body exercises and seated passing exercises or ball-handling skills can be performed with a doctor's permission. Attending practice and giving verbal encouragement shows support. Injured athletes can also help keep statistics, help scout competitors, and take notes on what is going well offensively and defensively. Athletes should always adhere to medical advice and follow therapy and exercise prescriptions to get back to the court as soon as it is safe to do so.

CHAPTER THREE

HOW DO PLAYERS PREPARE
ON GAME DAY?

Maya Moore takes her place at the table. It will be a few hours before she takes the floor with the Minnesota Lynx of the Women's National Basketball Association (WNBA). She eats pasta and a salad, carefully chosen because these foods help her feel invigorated. The food will fuel her muscles, which have been developed over hours of weight-room workouts in which Moore focuses on high-rep, low-weight exercises to tone and strengthen her body. She pays careful attention to her lower body to help prevent injuries.

Mentally, Moore reviews other physical processes she has put her body through to be ready for game day. Moore knows that all this preparation simplifies her game day. It's a focus she has had ever since she was an eight-year-old running hallway sprints that ended with shooting a ball into a mini-hoop. Moore thinks about similar drills she has performed to the point of exhaustion. She purposefully pushes herself to practice shooting with this feeling of exhaustion because she knows that this is what her body will experience during the late stages of WNBA games. "I've tried to be very intentional about making sure my body is ready to go for every game," she says. "Step out on the court, and it's showtime."[42]

Maya Moore has worked hard to prepare for game day her entire career. This work starts in the off-season and leads up to her pregame routine before every game.

MENTAL PREPARATION

Sports psychology researchers agree that an athlete's mental state has an immediate impact on competitive performance. They also see a correlation between mental state and daily training. Routine can be beneficial to mental preparation. That's what Maya Moore was doing by working shooting drills into her training at the end when she was already exhausted. She wanted to practice that feeling so that when faced with it in a game, it would be routine.

Identifying emotions that help players function optimally is also part of mental preparation. Having a competitive attitude is a positive emotion in basketball, but too much of it can be detrimental to the team's effort.

> **"I've tried to be very intentional about making sure my body is ready to go for every game."**[42]
>
> *– Maya Moore, Minnesota Lynx*

Self-confidence, defined by one researcher as "an inner belief most often based on past performance accomplishments and the achievement of goals," is a predictor of success.[43] Whatever an athlete does as part of a mental preparation routine should help boost self-confidence. A player can create a highlight video showcasing his or her successes and achievements. This can aid as a self-confidence booster when viewed before a game. Creating a personalized video can be done by recording videos of practice or game segments and then editing and choosing clips that demonstrate a player performing at his or her best.

Because basketball is a team sport, sometimes individual players can feel like they have a lack of control. If players set personal goals as part of game-day preparation, it can bring a sense of control back to the player. Examples of game day goals might be setting a personal free-throw percentage goal, or choosing a certain number of assists or rebounds the player would like to reach during the game.

KNOW THE OPPONENT

Another key to mental preparation is knowledge of the opponent. Coaches will often obtain scouting reports or scout teams personally to try to pinpoint areas where preparation may be needed. They may obtain video footage for the entire team to watch. Then, as part of practice in the days leading up to the game, the opposing team's plays may be practiced so that the most effective defensive strategies can be found. Key players are identified. Details from this research on the opposing team, such as a star player's dominant hand, can help teams prepare strategies for game situations.

Building on knowledge of the opposing team's plays, players can then anticipate player movement. The keys to anticipation of any single basketball player's movement are all fundamental skills of good defense. Players should watch their opponent's core, instead of their head or hands. All players on offense either have the ball or want the ball. They may try to sway the defense with head fakes, jab steps, and pump fakes. But the player's core must move in the direction the player intends to go. To keep between the ball and the opponent, good defenders stay on the balls of their feet. This allows for faster reaction time, especially when needing to backpedal toward the basket. Another key factor to anticipating and defending player movement is to stay low to the ground. Bent knees will help a defender stay balanced and will allow for quick and short steps. As players fatigue, they tend to forget these steps. Running through a mental checklist of solid defensive positions can help players prepare to meet the opponent and be better equipped to defend against him.

On game day, it is a common occurrence to see players listening to music. They may seem to be focusing, perhaps meditating, but they may be simply allowing their minds to drift or "zone out." They may just be daydreaming. Research concludes that players who are most successful in their sport are also vivid daydreamers. Not only do they daydream, but they practice in their daydreams. Doing this allows the player to imagine himself or herself achieving his or her goals. Creativity is enhanced in daydreamers because in daydreams, players can engage in imagined scenarios and visualize everything that happens. If a player is about to take on a superior opponent, visualizing scenarios may help a player come up with more creative ways to approach the game. Cognitive psychologist Malia Fox Mason says, "By allowing your mind the freedom to roam, the chances that you're going to have an insight are much higher. It's likely that you are going to recombine pieces of information in a novel way."[44] With hours of focused practice behind them, basketball players can afford to let their minds wander and relax before the game.

PHYSICAL PREPARATION

Depending on what time a game is to be played and how long a warm-up period there will be, the amount of physical preparation before a game varies. One college-level coach says, "We might have an hour-long shootaround where we go over our stuff and opponent's plays. We'll go over our strategies and personnel."[45]

A pregame warm-up will include a combination of shooting, stretching, and offensive and defensive drills. During open shooting time, players should practice shooting from the areas they would most often shoot from during a game situation. If a personal goal is a certain free-throw percentage, a player can practice from the free-throw line. This is especially important when visiting a new gym. When the backboard is made of glass, having a wall behind it in a small gym helps the player judge the distance to the hoop.

Stretching before games is an important part of injury prevention. It helps prepare the mind and body to play.

But playing in large arenas where the seating behind the backboard is much farther back can change the perception of the distance. The backboard's regulation size is 6 feet (1.8 m) wide by 3.5 feet (1.06 m) tall. The orange rim will be centered on the backboard, but visual perception in a new environment can be intimidating to players.

The 1986 basketball movie *Hoosiers* has a scene in which the basketball team from the fictional small town of Hickory, Indiana, walks into the arena where they will play for the state title. The coach has the team measure the distance from the basket to the free-throw line and the distance from the hoop rim to the floor. To the relief of his players, the coach concludes by saying, "I think you'll find it's the exact same measurements as our gym back in Hickory."[46]

GAME DAY NUTRITION

Nervousness prior to playing an important game may inhibit hunger pangs, but it is still important to eat. Carbohydrate loading before a game is one of the longest-standing sports nutrition tips. But to be effective the carbohydrates, which take time for the body to process, must be ingested approximately four hours before game time. As the carbohydrates metabolize, a substance called glycogen is stored in muscle tissue. Muscle only has a capacity to store a certain amount of glycogen. When playing a high intensity game, this stored glycogen serves as a fuel reserve for hard-working muscles.

Adding protein to pregame carbohydrates has an added benefit. Protein has been shown to increase endurance levels when ingested with carbohydrates. Protein also helps build muscle. A college coach says, "We try to eat a few hours before the game. Sometimes that would be a spaghetti marinara with chicken to get some long-lasting carbs with protein in there."[47]

Multiple studies have shown that during a game it is beneficial to ingest more carbohydrates to keep blood sugar levels even and to keep the stored glycogen ready in case the body needs it. This does not mean eating a piece of bread during a time-out. Rather, popular sports drinks contain carbohydrates. Another way to add carbohydrates is by eating fruit. During halftime, players can eat apple slices, pears, oranges, or grapes. These types of fruit may also be ingested if a player feels hungry just prior to game time.

Postgame eating should include a combination of carbohydrates and protein because this combination aids in muscle recovery and reduces soreness. It is recommended that this be done approximately thirty minutes after the game. Drinking chocolate milk after games is another popular choice. Because of its high carbohydrate and protein

Having a strong home-court advantage can help a team in many ways. Teams are more comfortable at home, have more fans rooting for them, and did not have to travel for the game.

content, it has proven to be just as effective as sports drinks. For athletes still growing, using chocolate milk as a postgame recovery drink can also add a bone-building source of calcium to the diet.

THE TRAVELING BASKETBALL PLAYER

While many teams and leagues keep players relatively close to home, there are others, especially at the collegiate level, that travel great distances to compete. Those athletes require special considerations.

Traveling means hotel stays and restaurant food. It means the daily routines of practicing at a certain time and a certain place are gone. These components will impact critical parts of pregame preparation.

If airplane travel is involved, the low humidity level in the cabin means there is also an increased risk of dehydration.

To combat these detrimental aspects, coaches and players can implement several helpful ideas. When staying at a hotel, they can set a bedtime curfew. Many hotels provide room-darkening window coverings. These can assist in helping athletes get the rest they need. Players can also make wise choices when eating at restaurants. Greasy food can cause stomach discomfort. Depending on the length of stay, bring as many food supplies from home as possible. Make sure the hotel rooms have refrigerators. Travelers can also be sure to drink plenty of liquids. Dehydration may be more pronounced with air travel, but any travel can put the body at risk for dehydration.

If a team is crossing multiple time zones, adjustment time is needed for the body. While many gyms may have air conditioning, players should be prepared to play in any situation. High humidity in a gym means there is high water content in the air and a player's sweat does not evaporate as quickly. This can cause body temperatures to rise. Playing in a higher altitude means air density is lower and less oxygen is available in each breath. Altitude changes can impact a player's breathing capabilities, and players may feel as if they cannot catch their breath.

Altitude may even affect the way the ball moves through the air. A study conducted in 2011 posed the question, "Does altitude affect free-throw percentage?"[48] Free-throw percentages of visiting players in Salt Lake City, Utah, and Denver, Colorado, were compared with free-throw percentages of the same players in lower altitude situations. Although the author realizes there could be other factors, such as fatigue, the study concluded, "The fact that nearly every comparison between arenas found lower free-throw percentages in

Salt Lake City and Denver indicates that it is very possible that altitude is altering shots."[49]

Teams talk about having the "home-court advantage." This means the home team will have more fans cheering them on. Depending on the size and shape of the gym, crowd noise and actions can impact players, especially visiting athletes. Think of a basketball player shooting a free throw. Opposing fans wave arms, towels, and whatever else is available to disrupt the shooter's concentration. Sports writer Jon Bois set out to determine how many more games a team would win if they could play all their games at home. He says, "Based on the number of games an average NBA team won at home over the past three years, it projects to have won 10.11 percent more games if it were allowed to play all its contests at home. To extend this example: this advantage would transform a 41-win team into a 45-win team. That isn't an enormous improvement, but it might just be enough to shove a team into the playoffs."[50] In a regular basketball season, it is not possible to play all games at a team's home gym. Players should take advantage of home games when they happen. They should also mentally prepare themselves for crowd noise when visiting opposing teams' facilities.

TEAMWORK

In 2015–16, the NBA's Golden State Warriors were on a mission to win seventy-three games in one eighty-two game season. That would break the

> **"Based on the number of games an average NBA team won at home over the past three years, it projects to have won 10.11 percent more games if it were allowed to play all its contests at home."[50]**
>
> *– Jon Bois, sports writer*

THE POSTGAME ANALYSIS

Regardless of if the team won or lost, players should perform a postgame analysis. Postgame analysis is a teaching and learning tool that provides helpful feedback and builds on a team's strengths. It can be done by watching a replay of the game or by simply verbally reviewing the key events. Looking at an individual's efforts and reactions, as well as the interactions between teammates, can also help locate issues that need to be stressed and improved in practice. Coaches will stress what went well and who positively affected the game. Players should be honest about their individual and team performance. This is also the time to ask questions and communicate, always positively, about any problems teammates may be experiencing on the court. Every game is an opportunity to test a team. A postgame analysis will help teams assess how they performed and be more prepared for the next game.

previous record of seventy-two games, set by the historic 1995–96 Chicago Bulls. Stephen Curry led the Warriors, averaging 30.1 points per game. But he knew those seventy-three wins required teamwork. In his speech accepting the NBA's Most Valuable Player Award, Curry said,

> Every single one of us has different personalities and different roles on the team, but we have such a great combination that it's obviously worked, but I think we need to appreciate what we have right now. We want to keep it together, and obviously want to see the end of this year out and finish our job and achieve our goal, but I hope we take a moment every single day, when we come into the practice facility or come into games, to appreciate the bond that we have and how much fun we have going out there and playing every single day.[51]

Each team member has a role to play. According to high school basketball coach David Wenzel, that is one of basketball's greatest lessons: "Players need to learn their role and accept their role. You push yourself through fatigue for the sake of your teammates, picking each other up even on the bad days."[52]

Coaches work to form relationships between teammates. Events such as team dinners or retreats may be planned. A college coach says, "We've done things like a preseason retreat where we talk about our core values. We share stories about ourselves and our lives. We discuss how we're going to go about being part of a team and how we go about this shared goal of being the best team we can be. We try to cultivate a brand of basketball that encourages sharing because I think that can raise the energy of the group and you can get some really special action out of people [who] feel that vibe and connectivity."[53]

TEAM LEADERS

Every team should have a leader. Team leaders, who may or may not also be team captains, often display common characteristics. In a study of NCAA college basketball athletes, researchers found that through their actions, not their words, these teammates have proven to be reliable in game situations, they are quality citizens both on and off the court, and they are willing to sacrifice their individual goals for the sake of the team. These characteristics result in the gained respect and trust players need to have in team leaders.

With confidence in their team leaders, a team's overall confidence level will improve. Researcher Daniel Gould says, "Research shows that team confidence is related to performance. Team confidence

Bench players should always be ready to go in. They can make a big difference in a game.

involves trust and confidence in one's teammates and coaches, as well as the individual athlete's confidence in themselves."[54]

The coach leads and teaches the team. Having confidence in a coach's ability to do what is best for the team may mean players need to check their attitude to make sure they are coachable as players. A coach cannot coach if the player refuses to listen.

IMPORTANCE OF SUBSTITUTES

Each team can put only five players on the court at one time. But due to the high intensity of basketball, substitute players fill an important role on the team. While sometimes these players are dismissed as simply sitting on the bench, or riding the pine, all good teammates realize their critical importance. Substitutes are called on not only to give a starter a break, but also because the substitute may have abilities that may match up well against an opponent. John Havlicek made it to the NBA All-Star Game three times before becoming a starting player. He understood his role coming from the bench. Havlicek said, "My job was to come in there and get the team moving."[55] Stressing the relevance of this position, the Sixth Man of the Year Award was established by the NBA in the 1982–1983 season. The NBA's 2018 Sixth Man of the Year Award winner was thirty-one-year-old Lou Williams. He averaged 22.6 points per game and scored 50 points in one game. His coach, Doc Rivers, said, "There are certain guys that are just professional scorers. He does it in every way. He's got a great ability to get fouled, to make shots through traffic. The key for me is to just stay out of his way. If he has a couple games where he doesn't make shots, I don't say a word because overall, he'll win more for you."[56] The most important thing a substitute can do is always be ready, physically and mentally, to be called on when needed.

A positive team atmosphere will form long-lasting bonds. A former Purdue University player says, "There are few things better than the bus ride home after a huge win on the road. You learn a ton about hard work and how committed you have to be. You learn what it means to fight through losses and difficult times with your teammates. You end up creating this group that's special."[57]

> **"There are few things better than the bus ride home after a huge win on the road. You learn a ton about hard work and how committed you have to be."**[57]
>
> – *former Purdue basketball player*

CHAPTER FOUR

HOW DO PLAYERS GET TO THE NEXT LEVEL?

When Michael Jordan was researching colleges to attend, he chose the University of North Carolina, not because it was going to be easy or because his family wanted him to go there, but because Jordan knew that a significant number of players who had played for North Carolina's coach, Dean Smith, went on to be drafted by the NBA. Jordan said,

> People were telling me I should go a different route, but I wasn't about to do that. I had locked in, committed to my goals. I wanted to know where I stood. I've always believed that if you put in the work, the results will come. I don't do things half-hearted. That's why I approach practices the same way I approach games.
> You can't turn it on and off like a faucet. I couldn't dog it during practice and then, when I needed that extra push late in the game, expect it to be there.[58]

Jordan says people like to look for shortcuts, but very few people achieve their goals by taking shortcuts.

FROM HIGH SCHOOL TO THE NBA

The natural progression in men's basketball has been to play and excel in high school, continue playing at the college level, and then be

Checking out a university can help students decide if they should attend that school. The campus and location are just two of many aspects a player needs to consider.

drafted into the NBA. But in 1974, a basketball player named Moses Malone shook up that mind-set when he decided to enter professional basketball after attending college for five days. The following year, two more players fresh out of high school—Darryl Dawkins and Bill Willoughby—followed his lead.

Malone went on to a Hall of Fame career. Dawkins played fourteen seasons in the NBA. But for Willoughby life in the NBA did not turn out as well. He played for six teams over eight years and left the league at the age of twenty-six. For many years afterward, high school players remained undrafted.

Then, in 1995, high school senior Kevin Garnett drew enough attention to warrant a workout in front of several NBA scouts. Standing at 6 feet, 11 inches (2.1 m), Garnett showed the agility of a much smaller player. He was an offensive threat anywhere on the court, and his size made him an imposing defender. He was the complete package. At the end of the workout, Garnett, who had given this tryout all he had, waited for the gym to empty and fell asleep on the court. Garnett was drafted by the Minnesota Timberwolves under head coach Bill Blair. Teammate Sam Mitchell says, "We had read about him. The thing that we didn't know was how intense, how dedicated, how motivated he was to become a great player. The very first practice we had, we kind of turned to each other and said, 'We're going to look back at this day and realize we played with a truly great player.'"[59] Garnett retired in 2016 having been named an NBA All-Star fifteen times.

High school player Kobe Bryant entered the NBA Draft in 1996. Bryant's father, Joe, had been a forward with the Philadelphia 76ers. At 6 feet, 6 inches (2 m) tall, Bryant was 3 inches (8 cm) shorter than his father. All the high school recruits before him had been taller and played in the center or forward position. Bryant was a guard. His decision to forgo college and enter the NBA was met with harsh criticism, as many saw him as overconfident. In a tryout for the Los Angeles Lakers, Bryant played against a forty-year-old retired NBA player named Michael Cooper. Dispelling any doubts about Bryant's talent, Cooper said, "He was playing like he had just graduated from college, twenty-one, twenty-two years old, and I think that was the most impressive thing about it."[60] Although originally drafted by the Charlotte Hornets, Bryant was traded and played his entire career with the Lakers. He retired in 2016 having won five NBA championships and been an All-Star eighteen times.

LeBron James was an all-state wide receiver on his high school football team. He also played basketball. With his size-16 feet and hands measuring 9.25 inches (23.5 cm) from the tip of his middle finger to the base of his palm, James had been able to palm a basketball since he was a sophomore in high school. Pairing this with his 6-foot-8-inch (2-m) stature, James has been a huge physical presence in the NBA. James stayed close to his Akron, Ohio, home when he was drafted by the Cleveland Cavaliers as the overall first draft pick in 2003. His transition to the NBA showed his impressive playmaking ability but also revealed that his jump shot and defensive capabilities needed improvement. James has shown continued improvement each year, the result of hard work, humility, and a sense of humor. Some predict that upon retirement, he will go into coaching. Nate McMillan, a coach who worked with James on the US National Team, says, "He understands the game so well, he could play all five positions if he wanted to. When you have that type of mind and then the talent he has, he could do pretty much whatever he wants."[61]

For Garnett, Bryant, and James, the transition from high school to the NBA proved to be wise and successful. But

> **"He understands the game so well, he could play all five positions if he wanted to."[61]**
>
> – Nate McMillan, head coach of the Indiana Pacers

Before playing for Team USA, Kyrie Irving played for the New Jersey RoadRunners in the AAU. Many great players have played for AAU teams.

many other players did not reach their goal of playing professionally. In 2005, the NBA changed eligibility rules regarding high school players. It stated that players must be a minimum of nineteen years old and must wait an entire calendar year from their graduation date to be eligible for the NBA draft. Although this rule has been hotly debated, it was still enforced by 2018. However, in that year, the NBA stated in a memo that it may change the rule as early as 2021. The WNBA has no age requirement for draft eligibility in women's basketball. Meanwhile, talented male high school players still have several options: play college basketball, go overseas to compete, play in the NBA's G-League, or stay home and wait one year.

HOW TO GAIN ATTENTION FROM COLLEGE COACHES

From Seattle to Miami and Phoenix to Philadelphia, when basketball teams in metropolitan areas go unbeaten, the press is bound to notice. *USA Today* routinely posts a top 25 list of high school athletes, including boys' and girls' basketball. They also keep an updated list called the "Chosen 25," which showcases individual athletes. The Chosen 25 is compiled by Jason Jordan, who bases the list on information from *USA Today*'s sports staff, recruiting experts, and writers. It is updated regularly. These players will be at the top of NCAA Division I college recruiters' lists.

In 1977, McDonald's sponsored its first high school All-American team. On that team was a teenager named Earvin "Magic" Johnson. He and his all-star teammates faced a team made up of players from Virginia, Maryland, and Washington, DC. The following year, McDonald's hosted its first All-American game with all-star players divided into two teams: East and West. Since its inception, the McDonald's All-American Game has showcased the most talented basketball players in the United States. In 2002, a girls' game was added. The proceeds of these games, which was more than $10 million as of 2014, benefit Ronald McDonald Houses, which provide free places to stay for families who have hospitalized children. Held each spring at the end of the high school basketball season, alumni of this game include current NBA players such as Kyrie Irving, Kevin Durant, James Harden, and Blake Griffin. WNBA players Seimone Augustus, DeWanna Bonner, Sylvia Fowles, and Brittney Griner are among those who were selected for the McDonald's All-American girls' game.

If a player does not fall into these elite groups, there are many popular camps where the possibility of getting noticed is increased.

National camps run by shoe companies such as Nike and Adidas are held in multiple locations around the United States. Even if players cannot travel a great distance, they can attend basketball camps at nearby colleges. If a player is interested in playing for a nearby college, that player should make every effort to attend those camps. This gives coaches an opportunity to see a player develop over the summer and, if a coach knows of a prospect who lives nearby, this might increase the chances that the coach will appear at a player's high school game.

Another way to stay involved in competitive basketball in the off-season and gain exposure is to join an Amateur Athletic Union (AAU) team. Founded in 1888, the AAU originally worked with amateur athletes to help prepare them for the Olympic games. Today, the AAU helps organize sports leagues, including girls' and boys' basketball, throughout the nation. Seasons usually run from February or March through July. AAU teams range in age from elementary through high school. Participation in AAU can be costly as teams travel for many games. The AAU does not have academic eligibility requirements, unlike school-related programs.

Since the AAU is a volunteer-based organization, it has met with controversy over placing the value on winning versus developing teamwork skills. There is great variety in the quality of coaches and how they teach the game, so it is important for players and their families to determine whether an AAU team is the right choice for them. Also, there may be many AAU teams to choose from in a certain geographic region. Families should choose the team that best fits the player.

In some instances, basketball players initiate contact with a coach they would like to play for by sending a video that showcases their skills. In addition, players can establish profiles and upload game

NBA DRAFT DAY

The clock ticks down and fans excitedly await the result, but right now there is no game involved. This is Draft Day for the NBA. The world's best young players sit nervously around tables as the NBA commissioner stands at a podium. Within a time limit, each team announces its draft pick. Emotions run high for players and their families. Those who had hoped to play for a certain team are drafted by another. Trades interrupt the draft announcements. There are always surprises. But for these players, they know they have defied the odds. They represent the 0.03 percent of male high school basketball players who make it all the way to the NBA. The odds are almost identical for female athletes in the WNBA. It is a responsibility and a dream all in one. A member of the 2018 NBA Draft class said, "I used to watch the draft and try to put myself in their shoes. To be here is just crazy." These newest players in basketball's most esteemed leagues become role models for future generations of basketball fans.

Quoted in "2018 NBA Draft Moments," NBA, n.d. nba.com.

footage on recruiting websites, making it possible for more coaches to access the information. But more often, coaches reach out to players. An NCAA coach says, "Coaches are out there looking at players: evaluating and assessing and finding players they think will be a good fit. Then they reach out to them."[62]

WHAT COLLEGE SCOUTS WANT

Besides solid fundamental skills such as defensive positions, shot selection, and ball-handling ability, college basketball coaches look for additional criteria. They may have certain positions in their roster they are trying to fill. Sometimes a coach comes to a game to watch a certain player and another player catches their attention. The things coaches watch for often go beyond basic statistics to include other factors. Brooks Thompson, a former NBA player and NCAA Division I coach, said, "My coaching staff watches players from the time they step off the bus until the time they get back on the bus. We watch how they warm up, how they interact with their teammates, how they handle themselves in competition, how they win, and how they lose. We evaluate the entire package, we don't just look at the box score."[63]

Coaches talk about a player's "court IQ." Being able to make decisions and react quickly to teammates in game situations with reliability is one of the most important building blocks of playing at any level. Players who want to play in college need to be able to work within multiple offensive and defensive systems.

In addition, coaches will interview people who know the player. "I talk to coaches. I may talk to the AAU coach, the high school coach, people that have coached against a player, maybe even someone who has taught them because we check the academics," says a college coach.[64] Coaches also check players' social media because it gives them an idea of the type of person they are recruiting.

> **"For me, it's always been a goal of mine to be the absolute best I can be, to take not only my game, but my teammates' game to that ultimate level."[65]**
>
> *– Sheryl Swoopes, Hall of Fame basketball player*

HOW TO CHOOSE THE RIGHT COLLEGE

Basketball may be a player's focus, but when playing at the collegiate level, it is important to think beyond the basketball season. Sheryl Swoopes was the first player to be signed when the WNBA was created in 1996. But earlier in her career, when she was a high school student looking at colleges, she talked about why she wanted to play for Marsha Sharp at Texas Tech University. She said,

For me, it's always been a goal of mine to be the absolute best I can be, to take not only my game, but my teammates' game to that ultimate level. I knew the fit was right, it was close to home, my family could come watch me play. Coach Sharp and her staff had done a remarkable job with the program already, and I knew it was just something I wanted to be a part of.[65]

Swoopes helped lead the Texas Tech Red Raiders to an NCAA Championship in 1993.

Swoopes touched on several important points. First, she had to identify her goal. For Swoopes, this was to play on a team at the sport's highest level. At the same time, a player attends college to graduate with a degree. When choosing a college, players should determine areas of academic interest to help determine if a college has academic programs and majors in these areas.

Swoopes was also interested in the staff at Texas Tech and her future teammates there. She knew this was going to be a team effort. This meant working together to accent each player's strengths. She knew coach Marsha Sharp and had researched the steps she had taken to better position the team for a run at the national championship. Swoopes trusted Sharp's coaching ability.

While some programs might be tempting because they are far away and a player feels they are ready to be away from home, it is still wise to consider the impact of being alone. If a player is accustomed to her family being in the stands to cheer her on, it may be worth considering colleges closer to home.

Depending on the level of college basketball, a school of choice may offer an athletic scholarship. Each school is limited as to how many scholarships it can offer per sport. Scholarships include requirements that players need to understand upon acceptance.

These can be both academic and behavioral. If a player is being actively recruited, a scholarship will most likely be offered to sway a player's decision. Even if a player is not offered a scholarship, it is important to keep goals, staff, and location in mind and then determine whether the school is affordable with the use of other academic scholarships, grants, and loans.

Being a college athlete reaps its own rewards. Besides working toward a degree, a former Purdue basketball player says, "There's a certain camaraderie and connectivity not only with your teammates and coach, but with the student body, alumni, and faculty. It's special in that regard."[66]

ALTERNATIVES TO COLLEGE

There are options for elite basketball players who want to continue playing after high school but do not opt to attend college. The NBA G-League, the official minor league program of the NBA, features players hoping to break into the highest level of professional basketball. Players must be at least eighteen years old. The NBA G-League holds an annual draft where undrafted college players, international players, and high school graduates gather with the hope of being selected by one of the franchises. All G-League teams are affiliated with NBA teams, and players may be "called up" during the basketball season. This means a G-League player under contract is signed by an NBA team under contract. Although the salary for G-League players is much lower than for an NBA player, many G-League players have successfully transitioned into the NBA.

Other players seek career options in leagues around the world. One former player who played in Estonia says, "It was very unique, fun, and exhilarating in its own way because everything is new: where

High school players can go on to play basketball in the EuroLeague instead of playing for a college team. This way they can improve and earn money before potentially entering the NBA.

you live, where you play."[67] Language barriers may be minimal as international players often know English. EuroLeague Basketball has teams in big cities and smaller towns throughout Europe. Whereas the WNBA does not have a minor league program, there is a women's EuroLeague. Both men's and women's EuroLeagues feature global competition. Many WNBA players spend their off-seasons playing in China, Turkey, Israel, Australia, and other foreign countries in order to make more money. So the level of competition remains high.

In 2018, businessman LaVar Ball created the Junior Basketball Association (JBA). Presented as another option for male basketball players who were too young for the NBA Draft, Ball's league paid players a small salary and offered playing time and visibility for hopeful players. Whether this new league will be sustainable remains to be seen. The top high school players in 2018 chose to play in college rather than join the JBA. Also in 2018, the North American Premier Basketball (NAPB) League, another minor professional league, was renamed to The Basketball League (TBL). In addition to these leagues, there are many regional professional and semi-professional programs players can become involved in.

Worldwide, basketball is played by an estimated 450 million people. It remains one of the fastest-growing sports in the world. Players are working through drills and putting up shots to get better and get ready for the next season's tryouts. It all comes down to a love for the game and dedication to physically and mentally preparing to play and win. The first step for any player who wants to improve is to simply pick up a ball.

HOW MANY PLAYERS GO TO THE NEXT LEVEL?

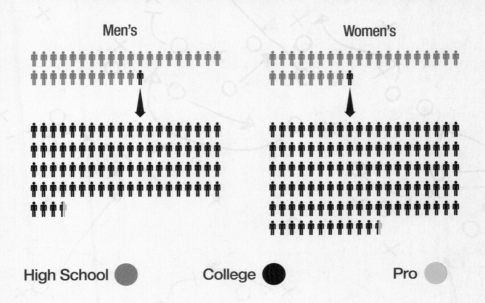

Men's

Women's

High School ● College ● Pro ●

According to the NCAA, there are more than 550,000 student athletes in high school that play men's basketball and more than 430,000 that play women's basketball. Only 3.1 percent of high school men's basketball players and 3.5 percent of women's basketball players will play in college. Of that 3.1 percent, only 1.2 percent of college senior players will be drafted by an NBA team. Only 0.9 percent of women's college basketball players will be drafted by the WNBA. Only 0.03 percent of high school players will play in the NBA or WNBA.

SOURCE NOTES

INTRODUCTION: DO YOU WANT TO BE THE BEST?

1. Quoted in Kirk Herbstreit, "At 16 Years Old, LeBron James Wanted to Be the Best in the NBA," *YouTube*, June 11, 2015. www.youtube.com.

2. Joseph D. Bates Jr., "Daddy of the Cage Game: Basketball Was Born Here." *Springfield College Archives and Special Collections*. https://cdm16122.contentdm.oclc.org.

3. Carson Cunningham, Personal Interview, September 29, 2018.

4. James Naismith, "Fundamentals of Basketball," *Springfield College Archives and Special Collections*. https://cdm16122.contentdm.oclc.org.

CHAPTER ONE: WHO IS GOING TO MAKE THE TEAM?

5. Michael Jordan, *I Can't Accept Not Trying*. New York: Harper Collins, 1994, p. 3.

6. Chris Ballard, *The Art of a Beautiful Game: The Thinking Fan's Tour of the NBA*. New York: Simon & Schuster, 2009, p. 139.

7. Cunningham, Personal Interview.

8. Quoted in Daniel Goleman, *Focus: The Hidden Driver of Excellence*. New York: HarperCollins, 2013, p. 163.

9. Quoted in Goleman, *Focus*, p. 163.

10. Goleman, *Focus*, p. 164.

11. Quoted in Emma Carmichael, "Do-It-All U-Conn Star Breanna Stewart Is Kevin Durant of Women's Game," *Sports Illustrated*, April 1, 2014. www.sportsillustrated.com.

12. Jordan, *I Can't Accept Not Trying*.

13. Quoted in Ballard, *The Art of a Beautiful Game*, p. 204.

14. Quoted in Ryan Kelapire, "Arizona's DeAndre Ayton Show Off 43.5 Inch Vertical," *Arizona Desert Swarm* (blog), September 25, 2017. www.azdesertswarm.com.

15. Quoted in Ballard, *The Art of a Beautiful Game*, p. 202.

16. Larry Lampert, "Exercise Your Eyes to Increase Peripheral Vision for Athletics," *Stack*, July 19, 2011. www.stack.com.

17. Catarina Abrantes, et al, "Long Term Effects of Different Training Modalities on Power, Speed, Skill and Anaerobic Capacity in Young Male Basketball Players," *Journal of Sports Science and Medicine*, March 1, 2006. www.ncbi.nlm.nih.gov.

18. Abrantes, "Long Term Effects of Different Training Modalities."

19. Quoted in Ross Simmons, "20 Stephen Curry Quotes Guaranteed to Motivate & Inspire You," *Hustle & Grind*, May 16, 2018. www.hustleandgrind.co.

20. Teen athlete, Email Interview, October 4, 2018.

21. Roger Kobleske, Email Interview, October 4, 2018.

22. Teen athlete, Email Interview.

23. Jordan, *I Can't Accept Not Trying*.

CHAPTER TWO: HOW DO PLAYERS PREPARE THEIR BODIES?

24. Quoted in Johnathan Abrams, *Boys Among Men: How the Prep-to-Pro Generation Redefined the NBA and Sparked a Basketball Revolution*. New York: Three Rivers Press, 2016.

25. David Epstein, *The Sports Gene: Inside the Science of Extraordinary Athletic Performance.* New York: Portfolio, 2013, p. 137.

26. Darren Burgess and Geraldine Naughton, "Talent Development in Adolescent Team Sports: A Review," *International Journal of Sports Physiology and Performance*, March 2010, p. 106. www.researchgate.net.

27. Rebecca Lobo, "Lobo: Dad Kept Me on My Toes," *ESPN*, July 17, 2010. www.espn.com.

28. Ronald J. Maughan and Susan M. Shirreffs, "Development of Individual Hydration Strategies for Athletes," *International Journal of Sport Nutrition and Exercise Metabolism*, 2008. www.semanticscholar.org.

29. Quoted in Abrams, *Boys Among Men*, p. 46.

30. Cunningham, Personal Interview.

31. Quoted in "Warriors' Arizin, Pioneer of Jump Shot, Dead at 78," *ESPN*, December 13, 2006. www.espn.com.

32. Quoted in J.A. Adande, "Secrets of the Skyhook," *ESPN*. www.espn.com.

33. Quoted in Adande, "Secrets of the Skyhook."

34. Cunningham, Personal Interview.

35. William C. Dement, M.D., PhD, and Christopher Vaughan, *The Promise of Sleep: A Pioneer in Sleep Medicine Explores the Vital Connection Between Health, Happiness, and a Good Night's Sleep*. New York: Dell, 1999, p. 369.

36. Naismith, "Fundamentals of Basketball."

37. Kobleske, Email Interview.

38. @DeAndreAyton, *Twitter*, September 6, 2018. www.twitter.com.

39. High school basketball player, Personal Interview.

40. Quoted in "Preventing ACL Tears: 4 Tips for Girls and Women," *Johns Hopkins Medicine*. www.hopkinsmedicine.org.

41. Quoted in "CDC Issues New Concussion Guidelines for Children," *Cleveland Clinic*, September 4, 2018. newsroom.clevelandclinic.org.

CHAPTER THREE: HOW DO PLAYERS PREPARE ON GAME DAY?

42. Maya Moore, "Maya Moore: For the Love of the Game," *Maya Moore – Official Website*, September 14, 2016. mayamoore.com.

43. Eric Bean, Daniel, M. Gould, and Ryan Flett, "Mental Preparation for Training and Competition," *Handbook of Sports Medicine and Science*. Chichester, West Sussex, UK: Blackwell Publishing, 2009, p. 57.

44. Quoted in Josie Glausiusz, "Devoted to Distraction," *Psychology Today*, March 1, 2009. www.psychologytoday.com.

45. Cunningham, Personal Interview.

46 Quoted in David Anspaugh, director, *Hoosiers*. Orion Pictures, 1986.

47. Cunningham, Personal Interview.

48. Bobby Samuels, "Does Altitude Affect Free-Throw Percentage?" *The Harvard Sports Analysis Collective* (blog), May 18, 2011. harvardsportsanalysis.wordpress.com.

49. Samuels, "Does Altitude Affect Free-Throw Percentage?"

50. Jon Bois, "Home Advantage in Sports: A Scientific Study of How Much It Affects Winning," *SBNation*, January 19, 2011. www.sbnation.com.

51. Erik Malinowski, *Beta Ball: How Silicon Valley and Science Built One of the Greatest Basketball Teams in History*. New York: Atria Books, 2017, p. 270.

52. David Wenzel, Email interview. October 11, 2018.

53. Cunningham, Personal Interview.

54. Bean, Gould, and Flett, "Mental Preparation for Training and Competition," p. 57.

55. Quoted in Bill Syken, editor, *Sports Illustrated Basketball's Greatest*. New York: Time Home Entertainment, 2014, pp. 119–122.

56. Quoted in "Doc Rivers Talks Blake Griffin's Injury and Lou Williams' Performance," *FOX Sports*, November 29, 2017. www.foxsports.com.

57. Cunningham, Personal Interview.

CHAPTER FOUR: HOW DO PLAYERS GET TO THE NEXT LEVEL?

58. Jordan, *I Can't Accept Not Trying*, pp. 14–15.

59. Quoted in Abrams, *Boys Among Men*, p. 37.

60. Quoted in Abrams, *Boys Among Men*.

61. Quoted in Ballard, *The Art of a Beautiful Game*, p. 210.

62. Cunningham, Personal Interview.

63. Quoted in Fred Bastie, "What College Coaches Look For in a Recruit," *USA Today High School Sports*, February 28, 2018. www.usatodayhss.com.

64. Cunningham, Personal Interview.

65. Sheryl Swoopes, "Back in Time: Sheryl Swoopes Reflects on '93 Championship Run," *Sheryl Swoopes – Official Website*, www.sherylswoopes.net.

66. Cunningham, Personal Interview.

67. Cunningham, Personal Interview.

FOR FURTHER RESEARCH

BOOKS

Kobe Bryant, *The Mamba Mentality: How I Play*. New York: MCD, 2018.

Brian J. Cole and Robert Panariello, *Basketball Anatomy*. Champaign, IL: Human Kinetics, 2016.

Matt Doeden, *The Final Four: The Pursuit of College Basketball Glory*. Minneapolis, MN: Millbrook Press, 2016.

Mike Lohre, *Six Degrees of LeBron James: Connecting Basketball Stars*. North Mankato, MN: Capstone Publishers, 2015.

Gregory Zuckerman, *Rising Above: How 11 Athletes Overcame Challenges in Their Youth to Become Stars*. New York: Philomel Books, 2016.

INTERNET SOURCES

Michael A. McCann and Joseph S. Rosen, "Legality of Age Restrictions in the NBA and the NFL," *Law Commons*, 2006. www.scholarlycommons. law.case.edu.

Danielle McDonald, "Basketball Stretching: 5 Benefits That Enhance Your Performance," *Basketball Trainer*, June 2014. www.basketballtrainer.com.

"6 Ways to Be a Top High School Basketball Player," *US Sports Camps*, n.d. www.ussportscamps.com.

WEBSITES

Amateur Athletic Union

www.aausports.org

This is the official website of the AAU organization. Use this site to find local AAU programs.

AthNet

www.athleticscholarships.net

This site offers tips for parents and athletes on how to get recruited and earn college scholarships.

Basketball Reference

www.basketball-reference.com

This website allows people to search former and current NBA, WNBA, and G-League players. The website includes stats and player information.

SportingCharts

www.sportingcharts.com

Find stats and information on individual NBA teams. Check the dictionary feature for definitions and explanations of the mechanics behind certain basketball moves.

INDEX

IMAGE CREDITS

ABOUT THE AUTHOR

Heather L. Bode started playing basketball on the outdoor courts of south Florida before moving to the gym scene in Wisconsin. In high school, her dad was her coach. She remembers spending a lot of time working on her jump shot during the summertime because, at a height of 5 feet, 4 inches, she was always looking for a way to get a height advantage on the court. After playing a year in college, she decided to concentrate primarily on academics. Today, she lives in Montana with her husband and five children.